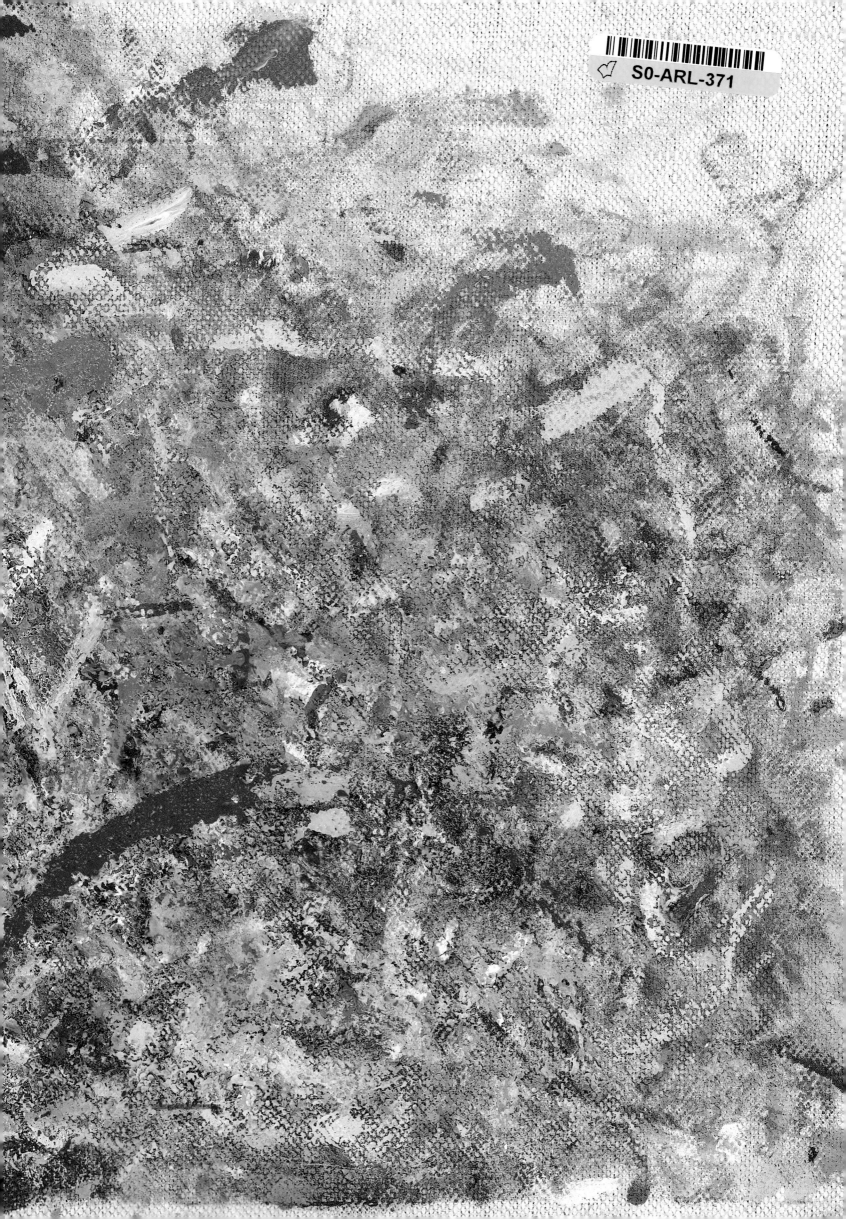

VAN GOGH

Mason Crest Publishers, Inc.
370 Reed Road
Broomall, Pennsylvania 19008
866-MCP-BOOK (toll free)

Illustrations copyright © 2000 Paulo Rui
Published in association with Grimm Press Ltd., Taiwan

1 3 5 7 9 8 6 4 2

Library of Congress Cataloging-in-Publication Data:

on file at the Library of Congress.

ISBN 1-59084-141-7
ISBN 1-59084-133-6 (series)

Great Names

VAN GOGH

Mason Crest Publishers

Philadelphia

Van Gogh lived only 37 years, yet his paintings lit the world. They shaped a concept of painting that led to the birth of modern art.

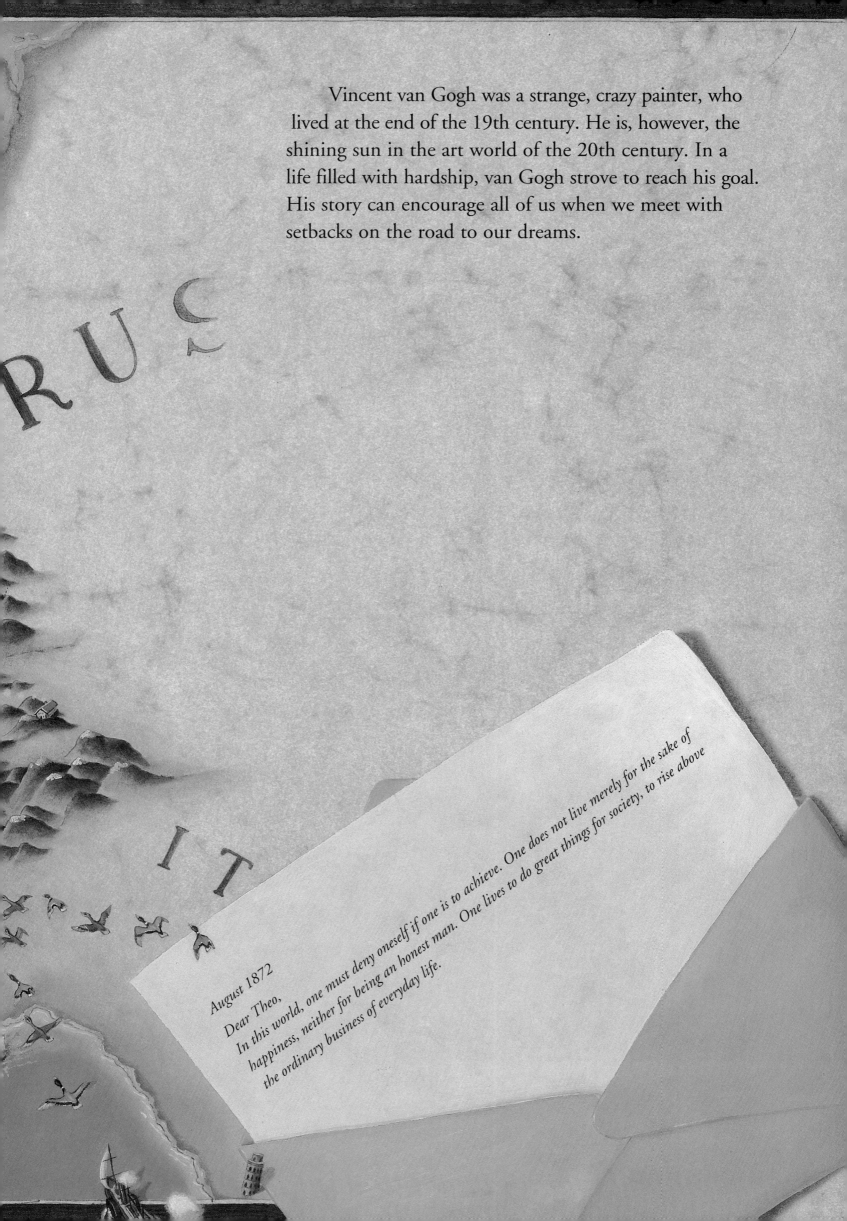

Vincent van Gogh was a strange, crazy painter, who lived at the end of the 19th century. He is, however, the shining sun in the art world of the 20th century. In a life filled with hardship, van Gogh strove to reach his goal. His story can encourage all of us when we meet with setbacks on the road to our dreams.

August 1872
Dear Theo,
In this world, one must deny oneself if one is to achieve. One does not live merely for the sake of happiness, neither for being an honest man. One lives to do great things for society, to rise above the ordinary business of everyday life.

Hello, everyone! I am Vincent Willem van Gogh. People simply call me van Gogh. My father was a Protestant pastor of a small church in Holland. Mother was a firm, stubborn, but cheerful woman. Both were kindhearted and loved God, but new ideas made them nervous. I was a rather odd child, and my parents worried that I might get into trouble. They did not understand me well, and I often argued with Father.

I was the oldest of six children. Of all my brothers and sisters, I was closest to Theo, who was four years younger than me. We often ran and played in the wheat fields and pine forests. Whenever we discovered something strange, such as a leaf, a bug, or a bird's nest, we would take it back home for further study.

I may have absorbed my spiritual faith and artistic energy from my relatives. On my father's side, they were either pastors who preached the gospel, or they were businessmen who bought and sold paintings. I had another family connection with a court bookbinder, a profession closely related to art.

As a boy, I enjoyed wandering through the forest and fields near home. I used to sketch the misty skies, the blurred shapes of faraway trees, grass, and wild flowers. I also liked reading. The writings and illustrations fascinated me. I was often immersed in books for long hours at a time.

When I was 12, Father sent me to boarding school. There I studied French, English, and German. I was terribly homesick. I did not get along well with my schoolmates, and I always counted the days until a holiday would arrive.

Then I would be able to hurry home to wander about with Theo and tell him about what had happened at school.

The three languages I studied helped me in my later life. I could read the great literature of Europe, and I experienced no language barriers in whichever country I visited. More important, I could write down my thoughts, feelings, and experiences, which in turn enabled others to understand me better.

When I turned 16, my family was in need of money. They lacked the funds for me to continue my education. I had to work to support the family. I was apprenticed to the Hague branch of the art dealers Goupil and Co., of which my uncle was a partner. Theo later went to work for the Goupil branch in Brussels.

I later became a primary school teacher of grammar, arithmetic, and spelling. I also worked as a clerk in a bookstore. I very much wanted to become a preacher and preach the gospel to the poor. But however busy I might be with my various jobs, I found time almost every day to sketch and read.

I would take hikes in the countryside or admire the works of great artists such as Rembrandt and Jean-Francois Millet in the art galleries. A whole day would pass without my noticing. As a result, I failed in every undertaking I tried. I had no money to send home and had to rely on my family for living expenses. Theo felt the weight of the hardship, since both the family and I depended on him. I was ashamed and angry, confused and frustrated. I asked myself, "Will I always fail at everything I do?"

I stared at the paintings on my wall and the sketch books that Theo sent me.

Van Gogh's concern for the poor can be seen in his early paintings. Throughout his life, he used his paintbrush to express his strong emotions.

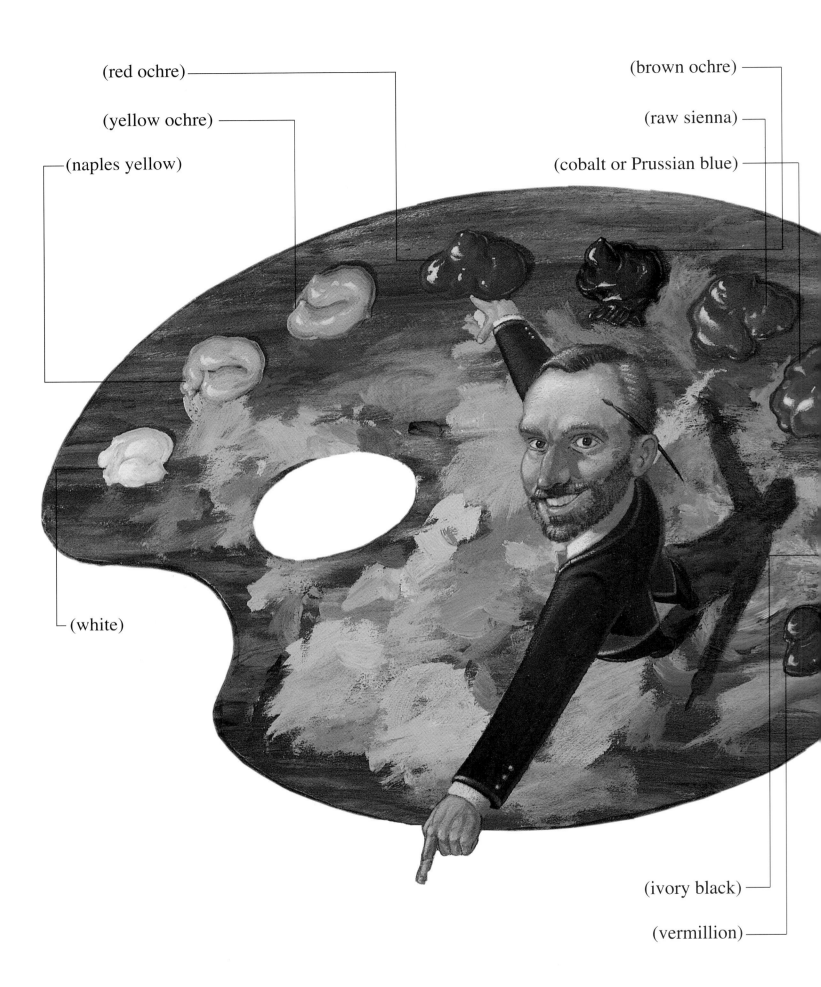

(red ochre)

(yellow ochre)

(naples yellow)

(brown ochre)

(raw sienna)

(cobalt or Prussian blue)

(white)

(ivory black)

(vermillion)

These are the colors van Gogh used to create his paintings. His work led to a style called Expressionism. This art style was less concerned with the scientific, natural world and more interested in the world of feeling and emotion.

I sat down immediately and started to write to Theo.

Dear Theo,

I told myself that I will take up the brush again and will really start painting now. I hope to say in my paintings words that would soothe me like music. From now on, everything will change for me. . . . Oh, Theo, my dear brother! Why can't you abandon the work in the art gallery and become a painter? I often feel that a great landscape painter is hiding in your heart.

After I decided to become a professional painter, I enrolled in a Dutch art academy for some time and learned the methods of painting from several Dutch painters. I painted with great diligence. I loved all the paints on my palette. They were enough to reproduce all the pure colors of nature. Gradually, the paintings I created possessed a greater and greater harmony of color. Eventually, I reached the point where as I was painting one color, I would already know what the color of my next brush stroke should be. I was never happier than when I was painting.

After finishing *The Potato Eaters*, I realized I had learned all that the Dutch art academy and nature could teach me. After more than a dozen years of loneliness, I looked forward to going to Paris and staying with Theo. Theo suggested that I go to the Cormon Studio to improve my painting technique. He said that Paris had quite a few intelligent painters who would be happy to guide me. I thought, "Ah, Paris! Here I come."

Theo was surprised when he read the note I sent him: "I'm at the Louvre. Come quickly." I did not follow the plan Theo and I agreed upon but came to Paris on the spur of the moment. I couldn't help it. I could not wait anymore. Paris was indeed an eye-opener.

There I saw the paintings of Hokusai Katsushike and Hiroshige Ando, representing the Japanese *ukiyo-e* (literally "transitory world pictures"), and the Impressionists. I remember the first time I saw an Impressionist painting. It was in a small backroom on the second floor of the Coupil & Cie Art Gallery. Theo did well at the art gallery. His boss permitted him to exhibit the then little-known Impressionist paintings in an out-of-the-way corner of the room.

How different they were from Dutch art. The Dutch paintings were usually dark and gloomy. They looked as if they were painted in candlelight after the sun had set. The Impressionist geniuses, on the other hand, painted in the transparent sunlight and air. They even painted blowing wind and light rays. They made nature and its endless variety lively and inspiring. Oh! How immensely powerful!

I tried changing the colors on my palette. I used a brand-new pair of eyes and a new soul to look at, experience, and paint the landscape and people of Paris.

During this period, I painted like mad. I painted models, and when I was too poor to pay for models, I painted myself or flowers or other "still lifes." I even painted the scenery outside my window. I wanted to paint as well as the Impressionist painters. In two years, I painted over 200 works. I was more and more in my element in the use of colors. But no one bought my growing number of paintings. My highest honor was to display them in the show windows of Tanguy. Theo did his best to help me and I did my best to paint.

What was the problem? I sincerely wanted to lessen Theo's financial burden and I also wanted to succeed. I was sad whenever I remembered that my work brought in no money.

French painters in the late 19th century were excited about their new use of color—but they were less serious than van Gogh. They loved to go to parties and drink too much wine; they danced and laughed and played silly games. Sober, intense van Gogh did not fit in well with their happy-go-lucky approach to life.

The dissatisfaction I felt for myself gradually developed into disgust for my environment. I felt the Parisian atmosphere was becoming more and more depressing. The artists did nothing all day but drink wine and conduct silly chitchats.

One day Henri de Toulouse-Lautrec told me that there was a place called Arles in the southeast of France. He said, "You will like that place. The light is crystal clear and the colors are fresh and beautiful. In all of Europe, this is the only place where pure Japanese-style crispness and brightness can be found."

One day in February 1888, I left a note for Theo telling him I was going.

When the train stopped at Arles, I saw clear bright skies, a lemon sun, and a beautiful pinkish landscape like a sea of apricot blossoms. My hands were shaking. How could I express these colors on my canvas?

I was awake for most of the night. The colors of Arles floated and swirled in my mind, and finally swept me into sleep.

Every day at dawn, I would take my easel and wander into the wild to paint from nature. The wind blew strongly. Even after sunrise, the air was so cold that it gave me goose pimples. I discovered that I was gradually forgetting Paris, all those theories regarding color, and those dull and silly chitchats.

Nature was teaching me, in all its honesty, all I needed to know about color and forms. I was like a painting machine gone into overdrive, churning out painting after painting. I did not know whether they were good or bad, but they kept appearing. Sometimes when darkness fell and neither the scenery nor my painting could be seen anymore, I would discover that I had not drank or eaten all day.

The daytime scenery attracted me; so did the simple charm of Arles at night. The bluish-black sky decorated with large stars

seemed to swing low under its own weight. The yellow light spilling out of cafes gave the night a feeling of warmth. The silk cypresses swayed in the wind. However, there were no lights outdoors in the night. How could I see to paint?

A few days later I came up with a good solution. I put lighted candles on my hat! But as I painted, I was in such a good mood that I often shook or nodded my head, which made the hot wax drip on my hands.

I seldom spoke and others seldom spoke to me. Spring went by and summer arrived. The residents of Arles saw me leaving for the suburbs before dawn with a lot of gear. However hot the sun was, I never wore a hat. I did not drink or eat for the whole day and returned after sunset, taking back with me painting gear and oil paintings that had yet to dry. Dirty me looked like a burned sweet potato with broken skin. They called me the "Red-Headed Lunatic." No one was willing to be my model, since they thought that I would paint them as strange animals of yellow, green, or red.

Though I spoke little, I did, however, write many letters to Theo, Toulouse-Lautrec, and other artists. In Arles, no one understood art and no one wanted to be my friend. It was only through writing letters that I could chat with friends in Paris and discuss my paintings, my moods, and my ideas. Of course, I also had to ask Theo for money to pay for my living expenses, even though I hated to do so. I could have stood being hungry, but I could not bear not having enough money to buy paint and canvas. For me, to go without painting would be to waste the life I'd been given.

After mailing so many letters, I got to know Roulin the postman. Roulin and his family were my only friends in Arles, and I painted several portraits of them. With Roulin's help, I found a house that was cheaper than the inn where I'd been staying. This place is now known as the "yellow house."

Paul Gauguin and I were good friends when I was in Paris. In October 1888, Gauguin came to Arles and stayed at my place. We planned to send Theo the paintings we finished every month. Before they were sold, Theo would provide us

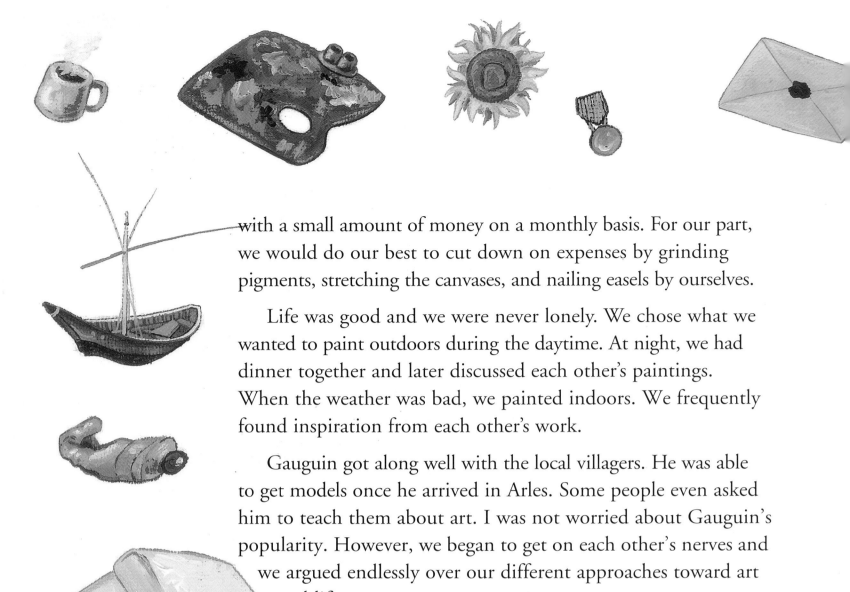

with a small amount of money on a monthly basis. For our part, we would do our best to cut down on expenses by grinding pigments, stretching the canvases, and nailing easels by ourselves.

Life was good and we were never lonely. We chose what we wanted to paint outdoors during the daytime. At night, we had dinner together and later discussed each other's paintings. When the weather was bad, we painted indoors. We frequently found inspiration from each other's work.

Gauguin got along well with the local villagers. He was able to get models once he arrived in Arles. Some people even asked him to teach them about art. I was not worried about Gauguin's popularity. However, we began to get on each other's nerves and we argued endlessly over our different approaches toward art and life.

"Vincent, I beg you, cover the paints and throw away the useless ones. Don't leave them lying around everywhere. How can we paint like this?

"No wonder you can't paint well. Look at these awful scenes. The colors and the brushstrokes don't match. What a mess!"

"You don't know a thing, Gauguin. I want others to understand that the sun gives its life to these flowers, grass, and trees, just like these flowers, grass, and trees give their life to the sun. You must first feel the pulse of all the things on

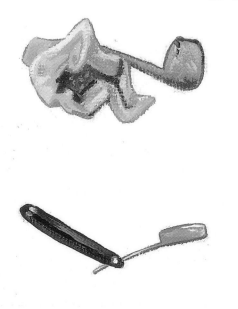

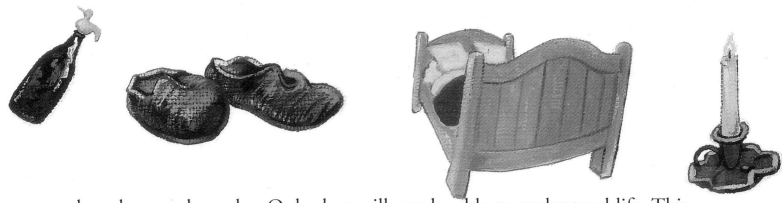

earth and everywhere else. Only then will you be able to understand life. This and only this is God."

"God, life . . . why don't you go back and be a pastor?" Gauguin's sarcasm and lack of understanding hurt my heart like a hundred needles. When Gauguin painted a portrait of me painting sunflowers, I said with a crooked smile, "Gauguin, you have made me look as if I am going insane."

I *was* really on the edge of madness. I would go out every day under a blazing sun and paint with every ounce of my spiritual and physical strength. Then when I went home, I had to listen to criticism and sarcasm. How could I continue to take this? Sometimes I wanted to kill Gauguin for being so proud, for refusing to understand me.

One night when Gauguin went out for a walk, I took a razor and followed him. Gauguin turned around and saw me. "Vincent," he cried, "what are you doing?"

The next morning when I woke up, I discovered that I was lying in a hospital bed. I felt for my right ear; nothing was there. I had cut off my right ear and given it to a woman I loved.

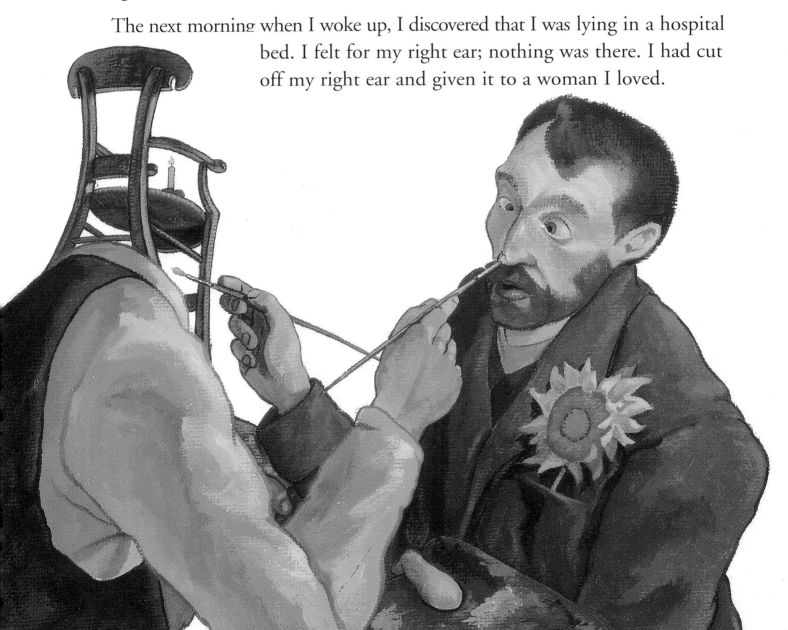

In the 19th century people who had emotional problems were often sent to special hospitals called "sanatoriums." These hospitals were often run by the Catholic Church, and nuns cared for the patients.

My neighbors were afraid that I might harm them. They wrote a petition asking the town judge to send the police to put me in jail. The doctors suggested that I leave Arles and stay for a while in the St. Paul Sanatorium at Saint-Remy-de-Provence.

The St. Paul Sanatorium was not far from Arles. When I first arrived, the people at the sanatorium would not let me paint because they were afraid that my insanity would return. Later on, I discovered that my insanity came and went in cycles. As long as I knew when it would occur, I could control myself. I persuaded my doctor to allow me to paint. During my stay there, I painted quite a number of paintings portraying the silk cypresses and the irises growing near the sanatorium.

The news that van Gogh cut off his own ear became headlines in the local papers. Now everyone in Arles decided that he really was a lunatic.

The sanatorium was another kind of hell where I suffered awful feelings of fear. I could hardly sleep at night and when I did I had terrible dreams. I wrote to Theo, and he said that not far from Paris was a quiet place called Auvers-sur-Oise where a kind doctor-artist could take care of me. I arrived in May 1890.

I was still sad and confused. When would people understand and accept my paintings? I was so lonely and depressed that each day only brought me more pain. I had been hurting like this for 10 years. When I thought of my unsold paintings in Theo's house, I felt as thought I could not bear the pain.

July 1890 was very hot. I shouldered my painting gear and went to the wheat fields. A blackish-blue sky hung low over my head. I could barely breathe. Suddenly, a host of black things shot into the sky, as if the sky had fallen. The black things flew toward me and I saw that they were crows. I slapped paint on my canvas. I knew I was losing my mind.

The next day I went to the wheat fields again. This time I took nothing with me but a gun . . .

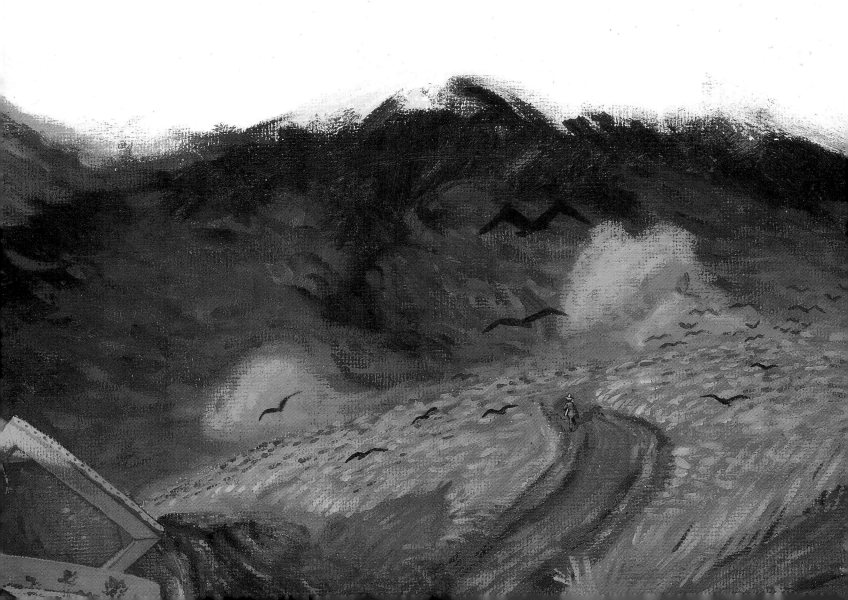

After his death, Vincent van Gogh's paintings finally gained the world's admiration. Today, his works are exhibited in museums around the world. One of his paintings, *Sunflowers*, was sold for $39,900,000 (U.S.). Van Gogh never dreamed that one day the world would come to appreciate his genius.

BIOGRAPHY

Author Richard Bowen resides in Wisconsin, with his wife Karen. He is the editor of *Spiritual Awakenings* quarterly and co-owner of Ariadne Publishers.

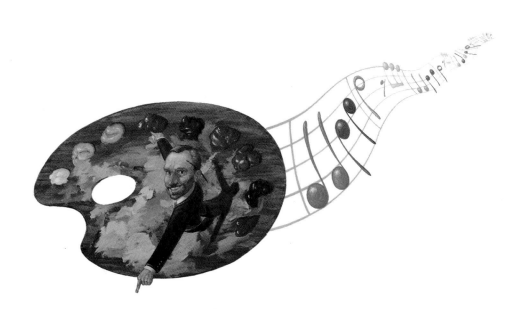

The Art of Van Gogh

▲Self-Portrait in front of the Easel 1888

▲Sun Flowers 1888

▲The Potato Eaters 1885

▲Still Life with Onions and Book 1889

▲Noon: Rest (after Millet) 1889~1890